KARISMATH
PRACTICE
WORKSHEETS

KARISMATH PRACTICE WORKSHEETS

SHAD MOARIF

Please go to our Companion website www.karismath.com for links to purchase the following set of Books on Amazon:

STAGE 1: Encoding Mathematical Symbolisms
STAGE 2: Encoding Conceptual Understanding
STAGE 3: Processing Numbers
STAGE 4: Mathematical Operations
STAGE 5: Algorithmic Thinking
STAGE 6: Problem-Solving

Karismath videos can be viewed at the site that explain Math concepts, procedures and operations while demonstrating how to teach them. All Karismath videos, from Grade 1 to Grade 5 are on every math topic and available as free streaming videos.

CONTENTS

The Karismath Practice Worksheets

I.   INTRODUCTION

The carry-on suitcase we use when boarding the plane, was originally designed (in mid-80's) to serve the needs of airline crew who needed mobility, compactness and manoeuvrability for their luggage. They had to hand-carry their luggage in and out of planes, where they used them, and lugged them through airports. When wheels were attached to their "attache-case", it was intended exclusively to address the needs of the airline crew.

However, since *all* airline travellers faced very similar inconveniences, this new novelty (wheels attached to the base of their suitcases) was extended to bags and suitcases of *all* shapes and sizes.

This is the Paradox of Specificity. The world of user research and experience suggests that products when designed to address the needs of a more specific group, such as those with math learning difficulties, prove to be actually useful to a much wider audience.

Unlike mathematics, school subjects like language or art lend themselves more easily to natural learning. Their content is a lot easier to understand because they are language-based or they use a tactile or visual medium (crayons, paint). The first is acquired from birth onwards, quite naturally; the second (art) via squatting toddlers clutching crayons, rubbing them playfully on a surface, provoked by the feedback of colors and forms. Beyond that, it is all about parental guidance.

It took many decades for their efforts to establish themselves as ways to guide children's learning. Today we can do it without coercion, without the need to control children's exploratory activities, especially during that critical period in their growth when physical movements morph into mental "moves".

Elements of early-childhood pedagogy evolved long before the term was coined for broader use decades later. When they finally spread into schools they were usually spearheaded by parents (often mothers) who became teachers. Decades later their classroom teaching led to the creation of creative, well-designed booklets, followed, decades later, by worksheets. This process of evolution was dominated by language learning-and-teaching needs.

Understandably so, since it is quite inconceivable to learn anything in print mode without acquiring solid literacy skills.

For mathematics, such a tradition is both sparse and rare. Innovative math worksheets have been developed more recently. Today they are as common as any other worksheet, and as diverse as the learning and teaching styles of those who design and use them. Serious and committed math teachers have well-honed pedagogical skills. When they unravel a math topic, they are able to pollinate their pedagogical practices with cues that provoke thinking.

It is a skill they acquire from their long and varied experience as practitioners. Teachers who understand math content fully well and know what impedes student learning, seek materials that serve their needs and those of their students. More often than not, they end up designing math worksheets at home.

In classrooms, many draw imaginative visual templates on the board, gesticulate meaningfully to suggest invisible shapes in air, draw lines, arrows, and so on. Through all this they manage to embody the activities needed to stir their students' curiosity and ignite their inquiry. Often it is best done by first inquiring deeply into the learner's reasoning processes.

Although such guru teachers are few and far between, there are many with similar abilities and talents. They cherish those rewarding moments when their students' eyes light up with understanding. Who wouldn't wish for more of it? As it turns out, though, teaching becomes stressful if teachers also have to design, create and produce their own worksheets until late in the night, seated at the kitchen table, correcting students' assignments. When they find their students performing poorly, teachers hurt as much as their students.

The *Karismath Practice Worksheets* are the first of their kind, designed to address the needs of a growing number of teachers who aspire to put all their efforts exclusively into teaching. At the end of the day, *that* is their strength. When a pedagogy feels sound, intuitive and easy to apply, they can use their strength compellingly, effectively, purposefully. They know what to do with it. By the same token, if the pedagogy turns out to be ineffective, they experience failure and blame themselves ... or sometimes, the learners.

Pedagogical instruments and tools rely on carefully conceived design, tested for their efficacy and ease-of-use. Like dentists and engineers, musicians and sports-persons, teachers are not expected to produce the instruments they need to practice their profession. They trust other professionals who specialize in their field and know how to design them.

Those professionals are expected to possess a deep and extensive knowledge of what dentists, musicians or teachers need. They are expected to understand and apply them in their own respective fields as designers, creators and innovators.

The *Karismath Practice Worksheets* blend pedagogical knowledge with instructional design using the principles of UDL (Universal Design in Learning). UDL principles require the design to be universal in the sense that those who feel cognitively or culturally disadvantaged will be able to do the exercises with almost the same ease (though varying speeds and accuracy at the beginning) as those who are advantaged or gifted.

Five streams of practitioner knowledge flow into their design:

1. Recent findings from experimental neuro-cognition research on how children develop their number-sense from birth onwards i.e. from the Approximate Number System (**ANS**) to the Natural Number System (**NNS**)
2. Extensive clinical practice and research conducted by the designer/practitioner during his 38 years of work with children and adults with math-learning difficulties.
3. A sound, workable knowledge of learning theories
4. A working knowledge of educational/child psychology
5. Instructional technology.

Mathematics teachers are not expected to have this kind of specialist knowledge to teach successfully in their classrooms—no more than pianists need the knowledge to construct a piano in their garage—in order to play it well. What they need is the tool, the medium, the instrument that is designed for a specific use until mastery may be achieved. Likewise, all teachers need worksheets in which the pedagogy is grafted like a plan inside the seed, a plan that helps the seed to sprout.

Karismath Practice Worksheets 1, 2 and *3* are intended for multidisciplinary professionals in Math education: (i) Master-Trainers (ii) Teachers (iii) Education Assessment specialists as well as school students, home-schooled or otherwise. They are also intended for use by interested parents or University/college students aspiring to become Math teachers. The Worksheets follow the generic principle of *shallow-to-deep, low-to-high, simple-to-complex.*

II. THE KARISMATH PRACTICE WORKSHEETS – A

Topics

A-1: Before-After Exercises
A-2: Number Sense Exercises
A-3: Counting Numbers
A-4: Making Numbers -10's

The topic sheets are designed to cover the age range 6 - 7 years or above as needed.

III. THE KARISMATH PRACTICE WORKSHEETS – B

Topics

B-1: Making Numbers (10's)
B-2: Making Numbers (100's)
B-3: Making Numbers (1000's)

Many of the problems that students encounter when learning the Four Operations can be traced back to a weak grasp of number concepts. *Number sense* and quantification are as intimately related as quantification and *number concepts*. Base 10 is the oxygen of quantification via groupings of 10. The construction of numbers via a process of systematic groupings suggest an early form of numerical reasoning. A complete mastery over this process invites the learning of Addition and Subtraction as intuitive and logical. It simply elevates numerical reasoning to the next level and ends up converting an earlier concept (Place Values) as an operation applied to learn future concepts (Add,Subtract, Multiply and Divide).

Making Numbers serves as the foundation to build pillars upon. The content is for learners aged between 6 - 8 years or above. The exercises also help to assess the early learning needs of learners of all ages who complain of math being "so difficult".

IV.   THE KARISMATH PRACTICE WORKSHEETS – C

Topics

Karismath Practice Worksheets-C covers the following three topics:

C-1: Writing Numbers
C-2: Practicing Ordinal Numbers
C-3: Comparing Numbers

The exercises are extensions of those contained in *Karismath Practice Worksheets – B. Karismath Practice Worksheets – C* advances learners' quantifying skills. The rational structure of the Base 10 Place Value offers, perhaps, the earliest exposure to mathematical thinking provoked by the grouping process. Learners learn to encode large quantities into large numbers.

Ordinal numbers are taught as part of the mathematical vocabulary needed when specifying placements of numerals during mathematical operations: (… the 3rd number, or before/after the 3rd number, every 2nd number … etc) or following instructions in everyday life (the 5th book on the right, and so on).

Comparing numbers is an important skill to learn since (a) it supplements the act of measuring and (b) provokes the **DKS**'s (Deep Knowledge System) ability to judge bigger, smaller, increase, decrease, difference, etc. and (c) generates the basic vocabulary needed for explaining mathematical ideas.

Between the three skills practiced in *Karismath Practice Worksheets – C*, learners attain the level of numerical readiness needed to learn, understand and apply the Four Mathematical operations: Add, Subtract, Multiply and Divide.

It is worthwhile to mention that the seeds of mathematical thinking lie inside a healthy, well- functioning Number Sense. Learners draw upon their more evolved number sense to enter the formal mathematical territory where seeds sprout. This is a major turning point. Children start to catch glimpses of mathematics dressing up in 'a formal attire' as it advances. It sprouts little stems, branches, then leaves and tiny buds.

V.   ACTIVITY SHEETS

Each of the chapters has been labeled "**Activity Sheets**". This is because almost all the highly scaffolded (visual) exercises are designed to invite the use of manipulatives or appropriate activities, as or when needed. These are very easy to develop using the cues in the Karismath designed templates. Most classrooms would likely have the resources.

Learners at this age (and older ones with learning difficulties) will find the manipulatives a useful springboard to leap from, before diving into their corresponding visuals in the worksheets.

VI. MANIPULATIVES

A word of caution regarding the use of manipulatives: they are essential during early years (3 to 7 years) since cause-and-effect relationships provoke tactile reasoning that are subsequently articulated orally as verbal reasoning. Their use begins to taper off from age 8 onwards. Numerical reasoning follows soon after numbers are introduced. However, numerical reasoning requires a more extensive exposure to manipulatives and these have to be designed thoughtfully, and to an extent, knowledgeably, to provoke cause-effect relationships that are quantitative. The worksheets carry all the cues for designing appropriate manipulatives if or when needed. However, that being said, it is important to help young learners enumerate quantitative relationships early by weaning them off their habitual over-reliance on manipulatives. It will activate their need to verbalize their quantitative reasoning.

Dyscalculic learners may depend on manipulatives and visual scaffolding longer than others. Likewise, there may be older learners who display initial ... often residual ... symptoms of an earlier cognitive defect in the ANS zone. Manipulatives can help explain mathematical concepts to induce numerical reasoning. Once they start to respond orally using numbers, other aspects of numerical reasoning are triggered and they spread quite rapidly. In all such cases manipulatives should be regarded as transitional environments to initiate connections between math concepts, symbols and operations. They would be enablers, or "self-starters" that ignite the cognitive engine.

VII. BRAIDED EXERCISES

Braided exercises are those that integrate *Content Knowledge and Pedagogical Knowledge*. This effect is incorporated in the exercises by braiding (entwining, wrapping) both of them around teaching practice.

Designing Pedagogical Practice

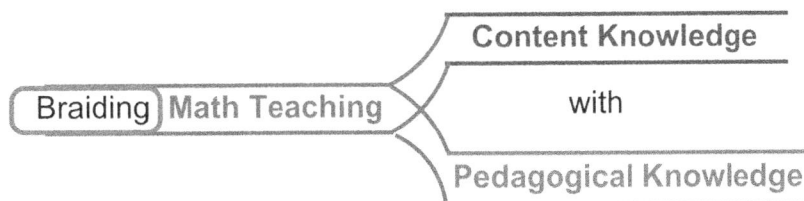

Braiding | Math Teaching → Content Knowledge with Pedagogical Knowledge

Braided exercises carry a cognitive load: they provoke thoughtful, reflective moments of learning target concepts and operations. They also lead to critical crossroads in student's early learning when they transition from ANS to NNS is anticipated.

VIII. DEMONSTRATIONS ON VIDEO

There are different exercise templates being used in this book. Most of them are heavily scaffolded and are designed to evoke visual, verbal and numerical reasoning. To understand these better, please go the Karismath website (https://karismath.com) and click on Teacher Training → (select "English") → Training Videos → Karismath Worksheet Demo Videos.

The videos introduce different templates and how to use them when teaching.

IX. CONCLUDING NOTE

Karismath Practice Worksheets-1, 2 and 3 help build the foundation of mathematical thinking, something that *all* math learners need. If they are offered better, faster, friendlier and easier ways to do it, they would much rather take that route. The topics extend across the age range 6 - 8 years or above. UDL (Universal Design in Learning) principles require the design of teaching-learning templates to be universal. In other words, those who feel cognitively or culturally disadvantaged will be able to do the exercises with almost the same ease (though varying speeds and accuracy at the outset) as those who are advantaged or gifted.

The exercises in this set of Worksheets (and in those to come) also help to assess the early learning needs of young children and those with math-learning difficulties. This implicates early detection and intervention. Those who find some exercises more challenging may need more attention, practice and encouragement. As it turns out, the incremental nature of the exercises, the gradual transformation of visual scaffolding into the most commonly-used templates for numbers, enable easy, resistance-free learning for all.

Users are advised to read "*From Math Anxiety to Mastery in 6 Stages: Stage 1: Encoding Mathematical Symbols*" and "*Stage 2: Encoding Mathematical Concepts*".

The books will help them develop sound theoretical perspectives and understanding of some new terms being used. Some of the exercises refer to encoding (when encoding a quantity, like "some" apples into its numeric symbol, e.g. 5) and decoding (when decoding the numeric symbol 5 back to quantity, to mean "five apples").

The Demonstration videos on the Karismath website sometimes use the term "*Deep Knowledge System*" (or DKS) which is explained in detail in **Stage 1**.

Trainers and teachers are requested to do the Worksheets themselves and assimilate the kind of practitioner's reflections they may provoke. By completing them, in conjunction with the books on Stages, they will be able to teach mathematics via new pathways to learning, those that do not fill gaps in learning, but simply remove impediments.

SHAD MOARIF
(Ed.M, Harvard)
Woking, Jan 15, 2024

MAKING NUMBERS - 10's

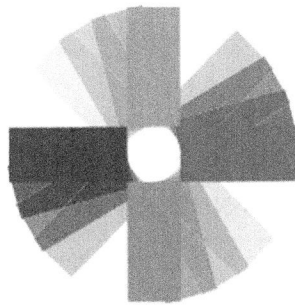

karismath

Turning Minds

ACTIVITY SHEETS

MAKING NUMBERS - 10's

MAKING NUMBERS VIDEOS

E. Using Place Values	1 Regrouping to make TEEN Numbers (Part 1)	https://karismath.com/video/44
E. Using Place Values	2 Regrouping to make TEEN Numbers (Part 2)	https://karismath.com/video/45
E. Using Place Values	3 Regrouping to make TY- Numbers (Part 1)	https://karismath.com/video/46
E. Using Place Values	4 Regrouping to make TY- Numbers (Part 2)	https://karismath.com/video/47
E. Using Place Values	5 The Turning Point in Regrouping (Part 3)	https://karismath.com/video/48

www.karismath.com

Karismath Worksheet Demo Videos

https://karismath.com/TeacherTrainingEnglish/5#l1

Encoding Quantities into Base 10 Numbers using Place Values - C

A

EXAMPLE

T	O
One Ten	seventeen ones

B

1	17

C

2	7

1

T O

Draw correctly

T O

Write in numbers

T O

2

T O

Draw correctly

T O

Write in numbers

T O

3

T O

Draw correctly

T O

Write in numbers

T O

4

T O

Draw correctly

T O

Write in numbers

T O

5 **T** **O**

Draw correctly

T **O**

Write in numbers

T **O**

6 **T** **O**

Draw correctly

T **O**

Write in numbers

T **O**

Write the numbers that follow:

7

Number	Words
10	Ten
11	Eleven
12	[ ] a)
13	[ ] b)
14	[ ] c)
15	[ ] d)
16	[ ] e)
17	[ ] f)
18	[ ] g)
19	[ ] h)

8

Number	Words
10	Ten
11	Eleven
[ ]	[ ] a)
[ ]	[ ] b)
[ ]	[ ] c)
[ ]	[ ] d)
[ ]	[ ] e)
[ ]	[ ] f)
[ ]	[ ] g)
[ ]	[ ] h)

EXAMPLE

T   O

Draw correctly

T   O

Write in numbers

T   O

| 1 | 0 |

9

O

Draw correctly

T   O

Write in numbers

T   O

[ ] [ ]

10

T O

Draw correctly

T O

Write in numbers

T O

11

T O

Draw correctly

T O

Write in numbers

T O

12

T O

Draw correctly

T O

Write in numbers

T O

13

T O

Draw correctly

T O

b) a)

Write in numbers

T O

Encoding Quantities into Base 10 Numbers using Place Values - D

EXAMPLE

T   **O**

How many Tens?   How many Ones?

7   13

Write in numbers

T   O

7   13

change to

How many Tens?   How many Ones?

8   3

Write in words:

How much is that?   How much is that?

eighty   three

Write in numbers

T   O

8   3

Read the number

14

T   O

How many Tens?   How many Ones?

☐   ☐

Write in numbers

T   O

☐   ☐

change to

How many Tens?   How many Ones?

☐   ☐

Write in words:

How much is that?   How much is that?

☐   ☐

Write in numbers

T   O

☐   ☐

Read the number

15

T   O

How many Tens?   How many Ones?

☐   ☐

Write in numbers

T   O

☐   ☐

change to

How many Tens?   How many Ones?

☐   ☐

Write in words:

How much is that?   How much is that?

☐   ☐

Write in numbers

T   O

☐   ☐

Read the number

16

T   **O**

How many Tens?   How many Ones?

☐   ☐

Write in numbers

T **O**

☐ ☐

change to

How many Tens?   How many Ones?

☐   ☐

Write in words:

How much is that?   How much is that?

☐   ☐

Write in numbers

T **O**

☐ ☐

Read the number

17

T   **O**

How many Tens?   How many Ones?

☐   ☐

Write in numbers

T **O**

☐ ☐

change to

How many Tens?   How many Ones?

☐   ☐

Write in words:

How much is that?   How much is that?

☐   ☐

Write in numbers

T **O**

☐ ☐

Read the number

Encoding Numbers using Place Values

T   O

EXAMPLE

19

Write correctly

T   O

1	9

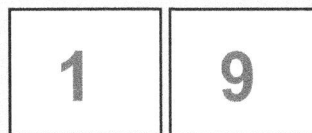

Write it in words

Nineteen

18

T O

11

Write correctly

T   O

Write it in words

19

T O

17

Write correctly

T   O

Write it in words

20

T O

14

Write correctly

T   O

Write it in words

21

T O

13

Write correctly

T   O

Write it in words

22

T O

16

Write correctly

T   O

Write it in words

23

T O

19

Write correctly

T   O

Write it in words

24

T   O

24

Write correctly

T   O

Write it in words

25

T   O

36

Write correctly

T   O

Write it in words

26

T   O

42

Write correctly

T   O

Write it in words

27

T   O

56

Write correctly

T   O

Write it in words

28

T   O

79

Write correctly

T   O

Write it in words

29

T   O

95

Write correctly

T   O

Write it in words

Encoding Numbers using Place Values

T   O

+1

2   15

EXAMPLE

Write correctly

T   O

3	5

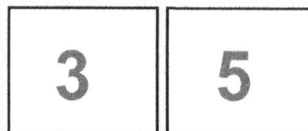

Write it in words

thirty five

30

T   O

2   15

Write correctly

T   O

☐☐

Write it in words

☐

31

T   O

3   18

Write correctly

T   O

☐☐

Write it in words

☐

32

T   O

5   14

Write correctly

T   O

☐☐

Write it in words

☐

33

T   O

7   17

Write correctly

T   O

☐☐

Write it in words

☐

34

T   O

8   19

Write correctly

T   O

☐☐

Write it in words

☐

35

T   O

6   11

Write correctly

↓

T   O

☐ ☐

↓

Write it in words

☐

36

T   O

7   13

Write correctly

↓

T   O

☐ ☐

↓

Write it in words

☐

37

T   O

2   10

Write correctly

↓

T   O

☐ ☐

↓

Write it in words

☐

38

T   O

3   11

Write correctly

↓

T   O

☐ ☐

↓

Write it in words

☐

39

T   O

5   18

Write correctly

↓

T   O

☐ ☐

↓

Write it in words

☐

MAKING NUMBERS - 100's

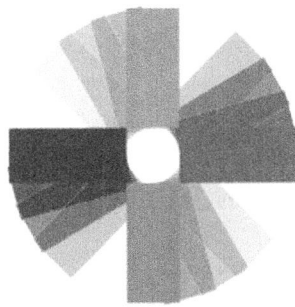

karismath
Turning Minds

ACTIVITY SHEETS

MAKING NUMBERS - 100's

MAKING NUMBERS VIDEOS

A. Making Numbers to 100's	1. Regrouping Numbers to 100's	https://karismath.com/video/71
A. Making Numbers to 100's	2. Digits and Numbers	https://karismath.com/video/72

www.karismath.com

Karismath Worksheet Demo Videos

https://karismath.com/TeacherTrainingEnglish/5#l1

Lesson Notes

Read aloud the following numbers

Tens **T**

2 **Twen**

Two-Tee

T	O
2	0

Tens **T**

3 **Thir**

Three-Tee

T	O
3	0

Tens **T**

4 **Four**

Four-Tee

T	O
4	0

Tens **T**

5 **Fif**

Five-Tee

T	O
5	0

Tens **T**

6 **Six**

Six-Tee

T	O
6	0

Tens **T**

7 **Seven**

Seven-Tee

T	O
7	0

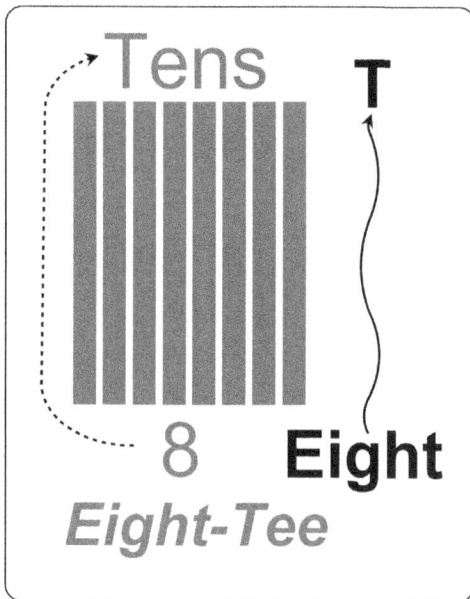

Eight-Tee

T	O
8	0

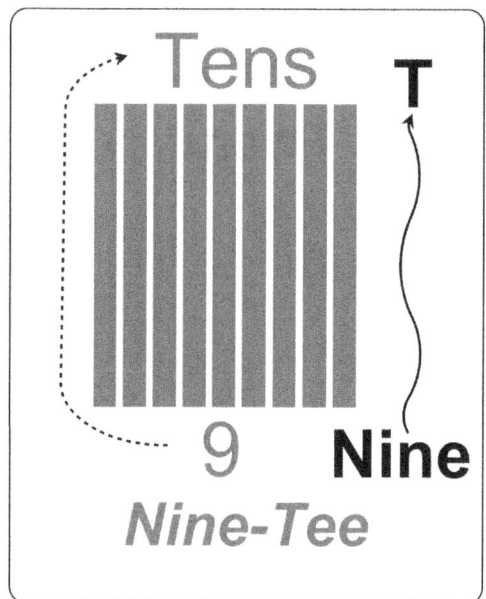

Nine-Tee

T	O
9	0

Encoding : Write the -ty numbers shown, in 10's

1 Tens

EXAMPLE

number *words*

20 Twenty

2 Ten

number *words*

3 Te

number *words*

4 T

number *words*

5 T

number *words*

6 T

number *words*

7 T

number *words*

8 T

number *words*

Encoding : Write the -ty numbers shown, in 10's

9

number   *words*

10

number   *words*

11

number   *words*

12

number   *words*

13

number   *words*

14

number   *words*

15

number   *words*

16

number   *words*

<u>Lesson Notes</u>

Encoding 100's

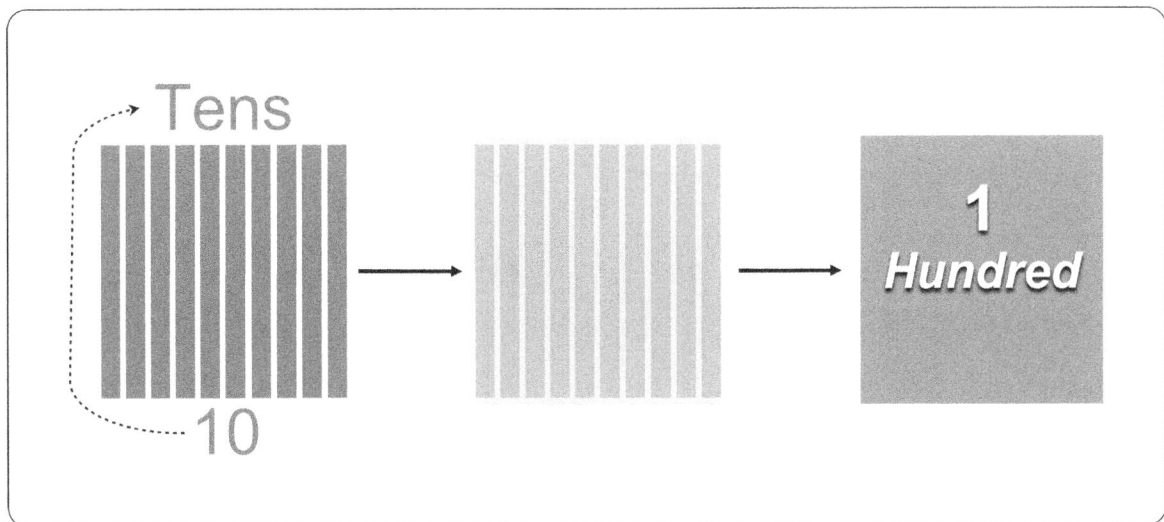

Write the numbers in Hundreds

17 EXAMPLE

number

300

18

number

19

number

20

number

21

number

22

number

23

number

24

number

25

number

Write the numbers in Hundreds and Tens

26 EXAMPLE

H   T

H : T
| 2 | 2 |

27

H   T

H : T
| | |

28

H   T

H : T
| | |

29

H   T

H : T
| | |

30

H   T

H : T
| | |

Write the numbers in Hundreds and Tens

31

H   T

H : T

32

H   T

H : T

33

H   T

H : T

Decoding Numbers as Digits

This number has
1 digit

9

Nine

This number has
2 digits

1st digit ➤ **1 9** ➤ *2nd* digit

Nineteen

This number has
3 digits

1st digit ➤ **2 1 9** ➤ *3rd* digit

2nd digit

**2 Hundrend
and 9-teen**

34

EXAMPLE

Write this number ?

H	T	O
	3	4

2

3

How many digits
does it have ?

Which is the
1st digit?

34

Write this number ?

H T O

How many digits does it have ?   Which is the 1st digit?

35

Write this number ?

H T O

How many digits does it have ?   Which is the 2nd digit?

36

A 3-digit number must have:

✓ check

i. at least 1 place value ☐

ii. 2 place values or more ☐

iii. exactly 3 place values ☐

A 3-digit number is always smaller than:

A 2-digit number ☐   A 4-digit number ☐   A 5-digit number ☐

37

Write this number

How many Place Values does it have?

☐ one ☐ two ☐ three ☐ four

Name the Place Values:

38

Write this number

✓ check

This number is a

A 2-digit number ☐   A 3-digit number ☐   A 4-digit number ☐

39 Write a 3-digit number in which the 3rd unit is 5, the 2nd unit is 0 and the 1st unit is 9:

H T U

✓ check

How many Place Values does it have?

☐ one ☐ two ☐ three ☐ four

EXAMPLE

Regroup this :　　　　…to make this:

T　　O　　　　　　**T　　O**

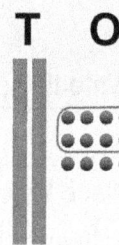

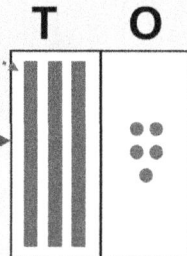

Write in numbers

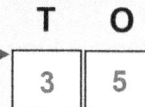

T　　O

| 3 | 5 |

Read the number

40 EXAMPLE

How many of these ● make one of these │ ?

10

Write its name

Ten

41

How many of these │ make one of these ?

Write its name

42

Regroup this :   …to make this:

T   O   T   O

Write in numbers

T   O

Read the number

43

Regroup this :   …to make this:

T   O   T   O

Write in numbers

T   O

Read the number

44

H	T	O

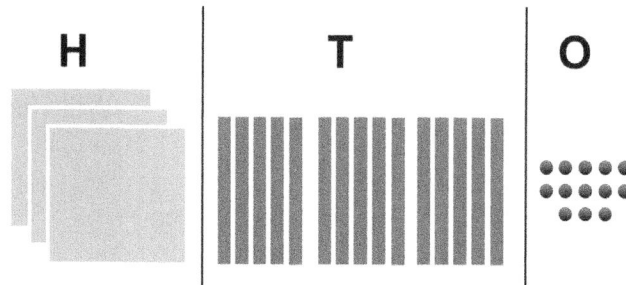

Re-group the above :

...to make this:

H	T	O

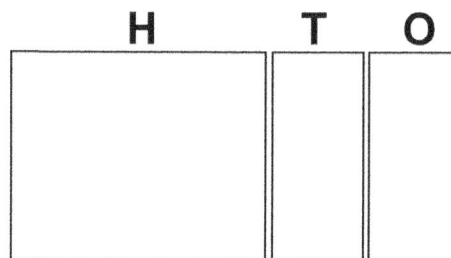

Write in numbers

H	T	O

Read the number

45

H   T   O

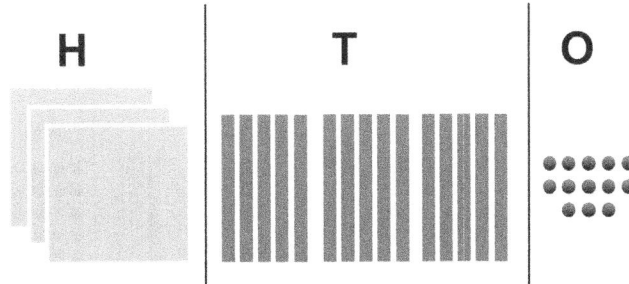

Re-group the above :

...to make this:

H   T   O

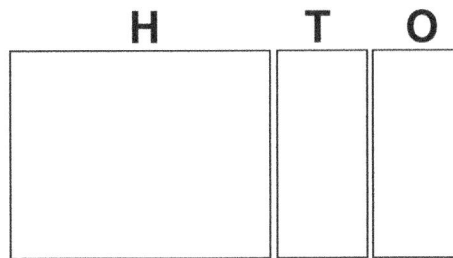

Write in numbers

H   T   O

Read the number

46

H	T	O
4	2	5

Read the number

Write in words

47

H	T	O

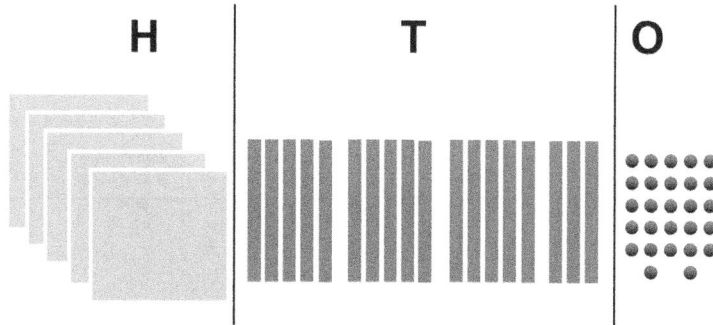

Regroup the above :

...to make this:

H	T	O

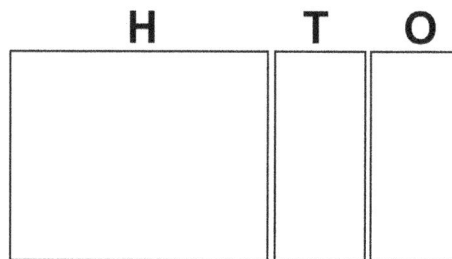

Write in numbers

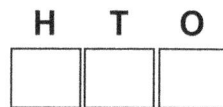

H	T	O

Read the number

48

H	T	O
3	5	0

Read the number

Write in words

EXAMPLE

Decoding Place-Value Placements - A

Read aloud as you fill the boxes

When there are <u>12 Ones</u>

H	T	O
		12

I write them <u>as</u>

H	T	O
	1	2

When there are <u>15 Tens</u>

H	T	O
	15	

I write them <u>as</u>

H	T	O
1	5	

When there are 12 Ones and 15 Tens

H	T	O
	15	12

I write them as

H	T	O
1	6	2

Read aloud as you fill the boxes

49

When there are <u>12 Ones</u>   H T O   I write them <u>as</u>   H T O

When there are <u>15 Tens</u>   H T O   I write them <u>as</u>   H T O

When there are 12 Ones and 15 Tens   H T O   I write them as   H T O

50

When there are 10 Ones   H T O   I write them as   H T O

When there are 18 Tens   H T O   I write them as   H T O

When there are 10 Ones and 18 Tens   H T O   I write them as   H T O

51

When there are 17 Ones   H T O   I write them as   H T O

When there are 13 Tens   H T O   I write them as   H T O

When there are 17 Ones and 13 Tens   H T O   I write them as   H T O

Read aloud as you fill the boxes

52

When there are 15 Ones | H T O | I write them as | H T O

When there are 18 Tens | H T O | I write them as | H T O

When there are 15 Ones and 18 Tens | H T O | I write them as | H T O

53

When there are 20 Ones | H T O | I write them as | H T O

When there are 20 Tens | H T O | I write them as | H T O

When there are 20 Ones and 30 Tens | H T O | I write them as | H T O

54

When there are 27 Ones | H T O | I write them as | H T O

When there are 19 Tens | H T O | I write them as | H T O

When there are 27 Ones and 19 Tens | H T O | I write them as | H T O

EXAMPLE

Decoding Place-Value Placements - B

H   T   O

+1   +1

2   15   12

Write correctly

H   T   O

| 3 | 6 | 2 |

Write it in words

Three hundred

and sixty two

55

H	T	O
2	15	6

Write correctly

H	T	O

Write it in words

56

H	T	O
2	15	12

Write correctly

H	T	O

Write it in words

57

H	T	O
1	18	4

Write correctly

H	T	O

Write it in words

58

H	T	O
2	13	15

Write correctly

H	T	O

Write it in words

59

H	T	O
4	8	15

Write correctly

H	T	O

Write it in words

60

H	T	O
1	9	16

Write correctly

H	T	O

Write it in words

61

H	T	O
5	11	19

Write correctly

H	T	O

Write it in words

62

H	T	O
3	19	11

Write correctly

H	T	O

Write it in words

63

H	T	O
1	7	25

Write correctly

H	T	O

Write it in words

64

H	T	O
2	6	30

Write correctly

H	T	O

Write it in words

65

H	T	O
8	10	10

Write correctly

H	T	O

Write it in words

66

H	T	O
4	20	30

Write correctly

H	T	O

Write it in words

EXAMPLE

Decoding Numbers into Quantities - A

Draw the Missing Numbers

67

Draw the Missing Numbers

H	T	O
1	5	

68

Draw the Missing Numbers

H	T	O
3	7	

69

Draw the Missing Numbers

H	T	O
1	2	0

70

Draw the Missing Numbers

H	T	O
2	3	4

71

Draw the Missing Numbers

H	T	O
5	0	7

72

Draw the Missing Numbers

H	T	O
3	5	6

73

Draw the Missing Numbers

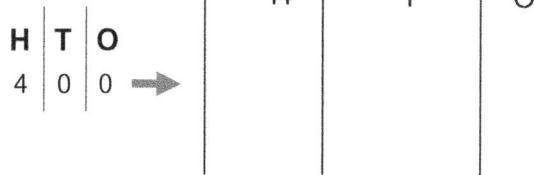

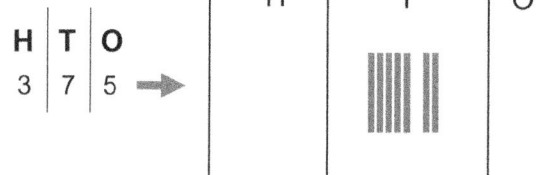

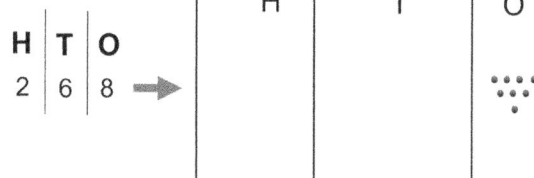

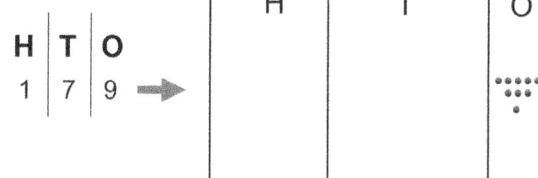

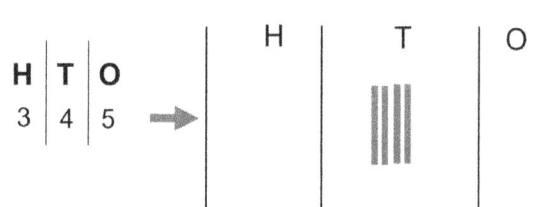

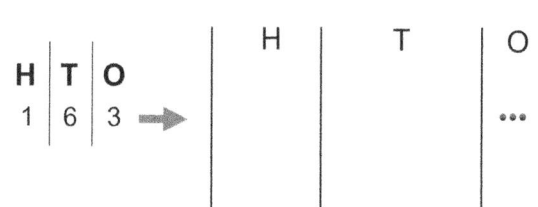

H	T	O
4	0	0

→

H	T	O

74

Draw the Missing Numbers

H	T	O
3	7	5

→

H	T	O
	‖‖‖‖	

75

Draw the Missing Numbers

H	T	O
2	6	8

→

H	T	O
		::::

76

Draw the Missing Numbers

H	T	O
1	7	9

→

H	T	O
		:::::

77

Draw the Missing Numbers

H	T	O
3	4	5

→

H	T	O
	‖‖‖	

78

Draw the Missing Numbers

H	T	O
1	6	3

→

H	T	O
		•••

EXAMPLE

Decoding Quantities into Numbers (100s)

Write the correct Number

H	T	O
1	6	3

H

T

O

79

Write the
correct Number

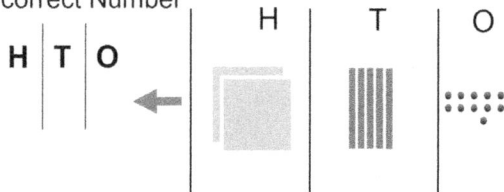

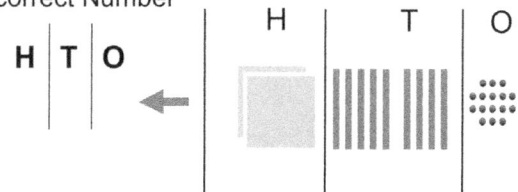

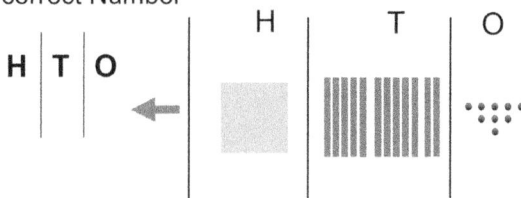

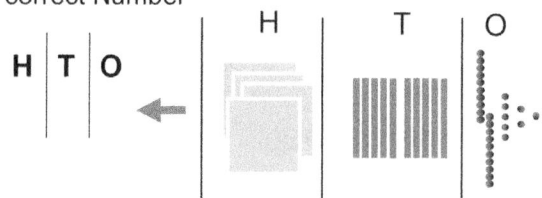

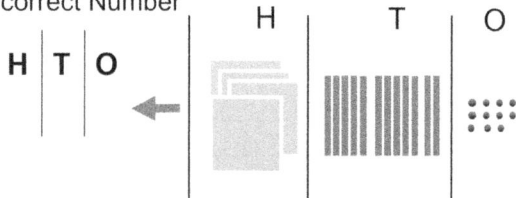

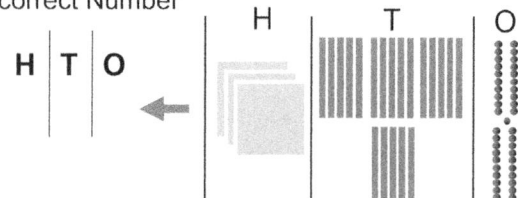

H	T	O

←   H   T   O

80

Write the
correct Number

H	T	O

←   H   T   O

81

Write the
correct Number

H	T	O

←   H   T   O

82

Write the
correct Number

H	T	O

←   H   T   O

83

Write the
correct Number

H	T	O

←   H   T   O

84

Write the
correct Number

H	T	O

←   H   T   O

Decoding Word-Problems as Quantitative Relationships (INCREASE)

EXAMPLE

Jim has this many apples		He got some more apples		He has this many altogether		Show as Numbers

Jim has this many apples and He got some more apples = He has this many altogether = Show as Numbers

T   O
[1] [4]

Show as Ones	Show as Ones	Show as Ones	Show as Tens and Ones
T | O ::::	+	T | O :::	=	T | O :::: :::::	=	T | O : :

85

Kim has this many oranges

and

She got some more oranges

=

He has this many altogether

=

Show as Numbers

T | O

| |

Show as Ones

T | O

+

Show as Ones

T | O

=

Show as Ones

T | O

=

Show as Tens and Ones

T | O

86

Tom has this many pears

and

He got some more pears

=

He has this many altogether

=

Show as Numbers

T | O

| |

Show as Ones

T | O

+

Show as Ones

T | O

=

Show as Ones

T | O

=

Show as Tens and Ones

T | O

87

Syma has this many bananas

and

She got some more bananas

=

She has this many altogether

=

Show as Numbers

T | O

| |

Show as Ones

T | O

+

Show as Ones

T | O

=

Show as Ones

T | O

=

Show as Tens and Ones

T | O

88

Katy has this many dollars

She got some more oranges

She has this many altogether

Show as Numbers

T | O

and

=

=

Show as Ones

T | O

+

Show as Ones

T | O

=

Show as Ones

T | O

=

Show as Tens and Ones

T | O

89

Bill has this many marbles

He got some more marbles

He has this many altogether

Show as Numbers

T | O

and

=

=

Show as Ones

T | O

+

Show as Ones

T | O

=

Show as Ones

T | O

=

Show as Tens and Ones

T | O

90

Amy has this many cups

She got some more cups

She has this many altogether

Show as Numbers

T | O

and

=

=

Show as Ones

T | O

+

Show as Ones

T | O

=

Show as Ones

T | O

=

Show as Tens and Ones

T | O

Decoding Word-Problems as Quantitative Relationships - B
(DECREASE)

EXAMPLE

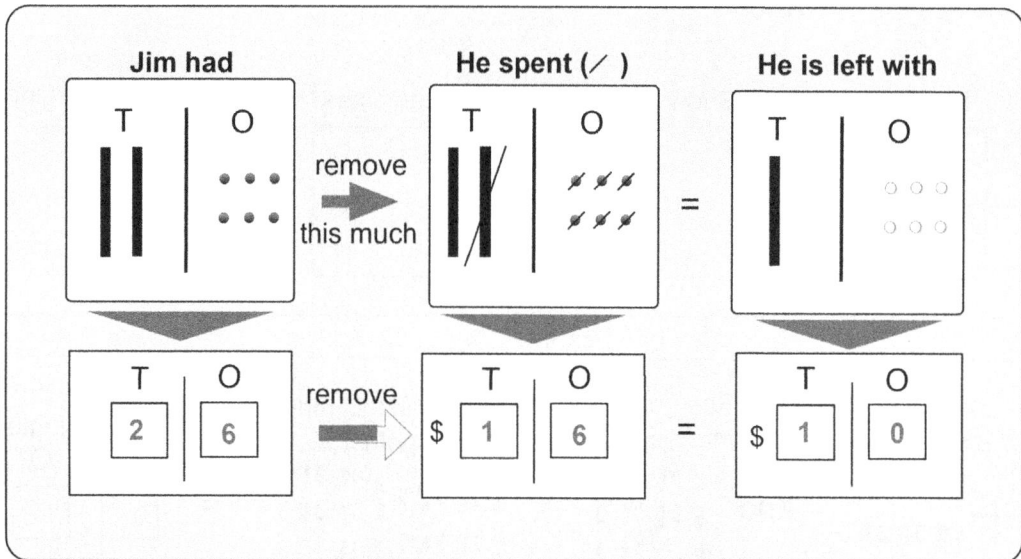

91

Kian had	He spent (/)	He is left with

remove this much

remove

$

=

$

92

Nick had	He spent (/)	He is left with

remove this much

remove

$

=

$

93

Ayesha had	He spent (/)	He is left with

remove this much

remove

$

=

$

94

Amy had	He spent (/)	He is left with

95

Kim	He spent (/)	He is left with

96

Tom had	He spent (/)	He is left with

Decoding Word-Problems as Quantitative Relationships - A (DECREASE)

EXAMPLE

Jim has this many dollars

H	T	O

He spent $120 on a video-game.

Cross out amount removed

Draw how much he spent

H	T	O

Jim has this many dollars **97**

H　　T　　O

Cross out amount removed

He spent $120 on a video-game.

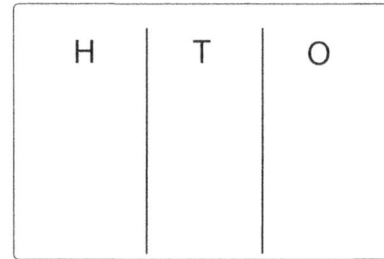

Draw how much he spent

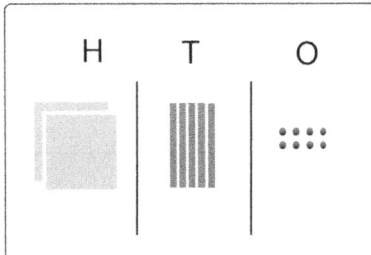

H | T | O

Kim has this many dollars **98**

H　　T　　O

Cross out amount removed

She spent $146 on shoes.

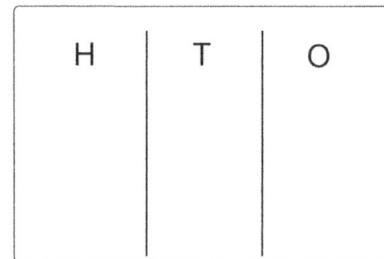

Draw how much she spent

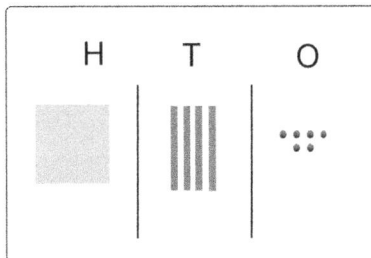

H | T | O

My dog weighed so many Kilograms. **99**

H　　T　　O

Cross out amount removed

She fell ill and lost 13 Kg

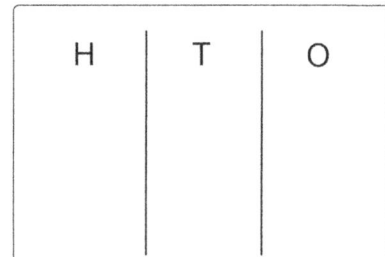

Draw how much she lost

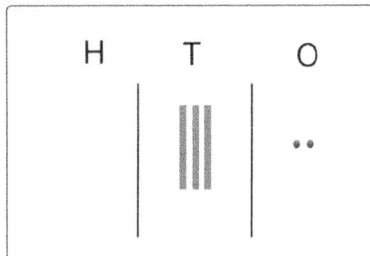

H | T | O

Molly had to drive so many kilometers **100**

H　　T　　O

Cross out amount removed

After driving 40 Km she stopped for coffee.

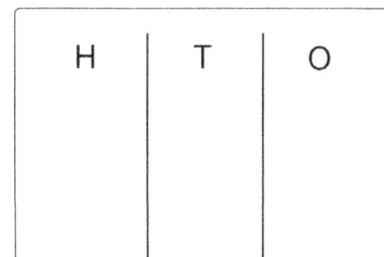

Draw how many km she drove

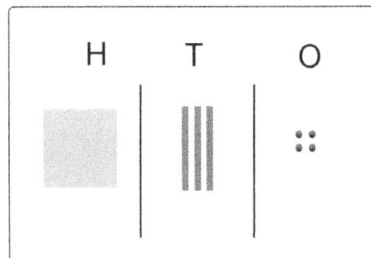

H | T | O

MAKING NUMBERS - 1000's

karismath

Turning Minds

ACTIVITY SHEETS

MAKING NUMBERS - 1000's

MAKING NUMBERS VIDEOS

A. Number Concepts	1 Before/After Numbers Part 1	https://karismath.com/video/140
A. Number Concepts	2 Before/After Numbers Part 2	https://karismath.com/video/141
A. Number Concepts	3 Grouping Humbers to Thousands	https://karismath.com/video/142
A. Number Concepts	6 Writing Numbers in Expanded Form	https://karismath.com/video/145

www.karismath.com

Karismath Worksheet Demo Videos

https://karismath.com/TeacherTrainingEnglish/5#l1

Lesson Notes

Encoding Thousands

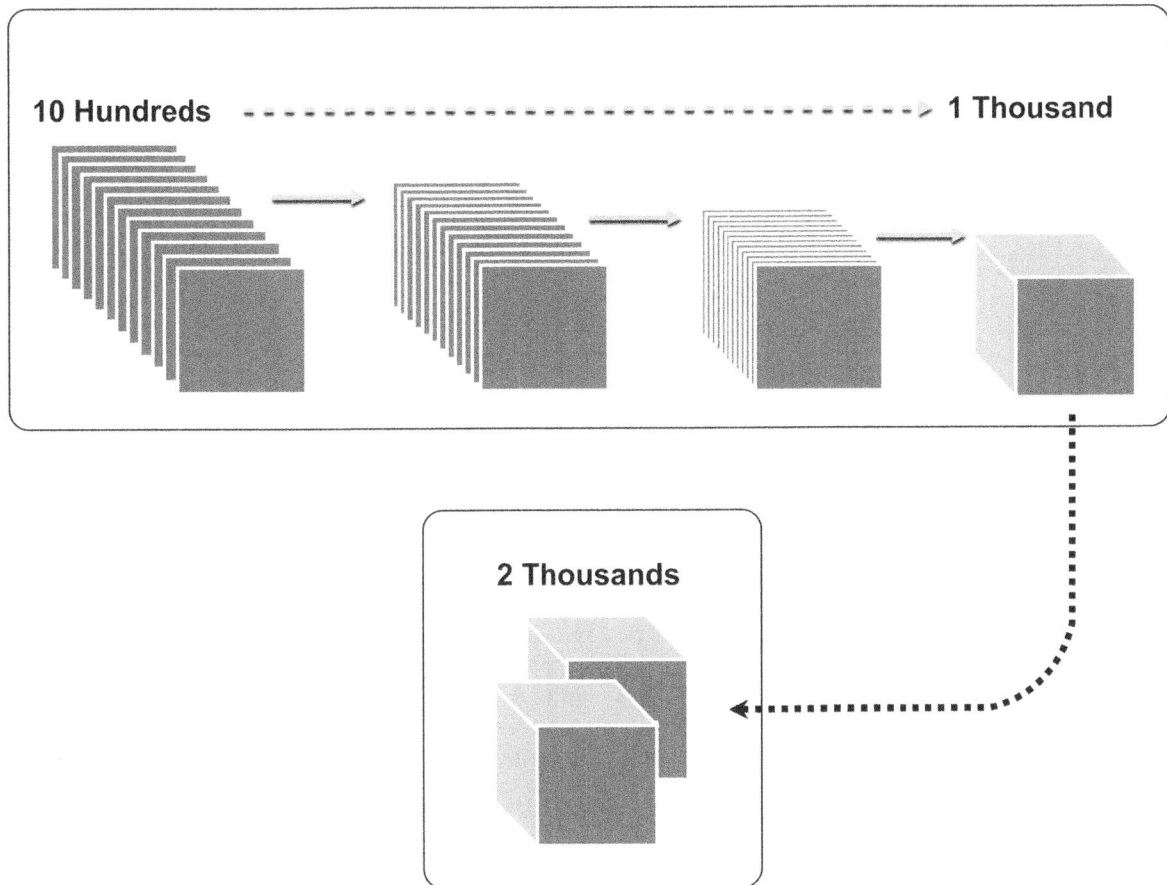

10 Hundreds -▷ **1 Thousand**

2 Thousands

Encoding Thousands

Write the following number in Thousands, Hundreds, Tens and Ones

EXAMPLE

Th	H	T	O
3	6	4	7

Write the number

Th	H	T	O
3	6	4	7

Read the number

(3 thousand , 6 hundred, forty-seven)

1

How many of these • make this | ?   ☐

2

How many of these | make this ■ ?   ☐

3

How many of these ■ make this ⬜ ?   ☐

4.

Th	H	T	O

☐   ☐   ☐   ☐

Write the number

Th	H	T	O

Read the number

5

Th	H	T	O

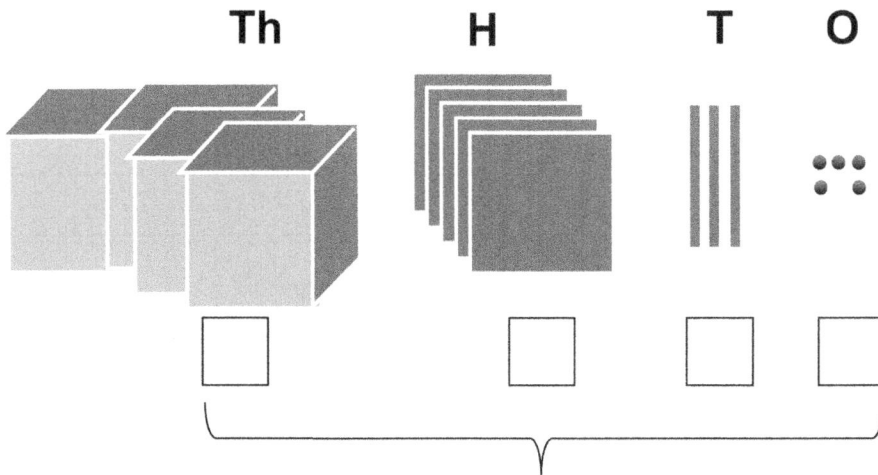

☐   ☐   ☐   ☐

Write the number

Th	H	T	O

Read the number

6

Th	H	T	O

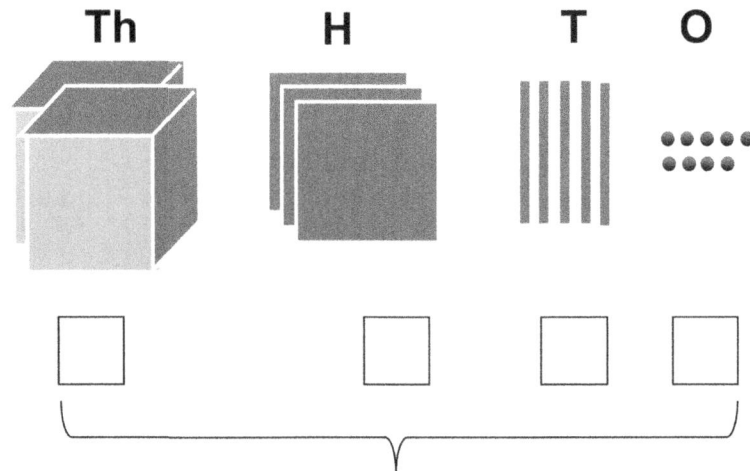

☐   ☐   ☐   ☐

Write the number

Th	H	T	O

Read the number

7   Draw this number: 4 2 6 8

Th	H	T	O

8   Draw this number: 1 5 2 6

Th	H	T	O

9

Draw: Two thousand six hundred and twenty-seven:

Th	**H**	**T**	**O**

Write the number

Th	H	T	O

Read the number

10

Write in words:

a) 3 582

b) 5 605

c) 8 019

d) 7 006

Encoding: Regrouping Place Values to Thousands

EXAMPLE

Th	H	T	O
3	12	11	12

Re-group correctly and redraw below

Regroup correctly and re-draw

11 Th	H	T	O

Write this amount below, using numbers

Th	H	T	O

Write in words:

Encoding: Regrouping Place Values to Thousands with numbers

Th	H	T	O
7	15	18	19

Re-group correctly

8	6	9	9

Write the number in words:

eight thousand six hundred

and ninety-nine

12

Th	H	T	O
7	15	18	19

Re-group correctly

Write the number in words:

....

13

Th	H	T	O
4	12	11	1

Re-group correctly

Write the number in words:

....

14

Th	H	T	O
2	9	11	19

Re-group correctly

Write the number in words:

....

15

Th	H	T	O
5	9	24	25

Re-group correctly

Write the number in words:

....

16

Th	H	T	O
8	19	20	31

Re-group correctly

Write the number in words:

....

17

Th	H	T	O
1	9	10	15

Re-group correctly

Write the number in words:

....

Decoding Exercises

18	Write the Value of **5** in each of the numbers below		
	3 5**82** 3 8**25** 8 3**52** **5** 382		

19 EXAMPLE

                5 6   4 9

Which number has more Units [ ] or [✓]

Which number has more Tens [✓] or [ ]

Which number is *bigger* [✓] or [ ]

20

                6 4   5 8

Which number has more Units [ ] or [ ]

Which number has more Tens [ ] or [ ]

Which number is *bigger* [ ] or [ ]

21

                4 3   5 6

Which number has more Units [ ] or [ ]

Which number has more Tens [ ] or [ ]

Which number is *smaller* [ ] or [ ]

22

                4 9   5 5

Which number has more Units [ ] or [ ]

Which number has more Tens [ ] or [ ]

Which number is *smaller* [ ] or [ ]

23

                7 9   4 7

Which number has more Units [ ] or [ ]

Which number has more Tens [ ] or [ ]

Which number is *smaller* [ ] or [ ]

24

                6 8   7 2

Which number has more Units [ ] or [ ]

Which number has more Tens [ ] or [ ]

Which number is *smaller* [ ] or [ ]

EXAMPLE

384 → 415

Which number has more Hundreds [ ] or [✓] (415)

Which number has more Tens [✓] (384) or [ ]

Which number has more Units [ ] or [✓] (415)

Which number is *bigger* [ ] or [✓] (415)

25

670 → 528

Which number has more Hundreds [ ] or [ ]

Which number has more Tens [ ] or [ ]

Which number has more Units [ ] or [ ]

Which number is *bigger* [ ] or [ ]

26

900 898

Which number has more Hundreds [ ] or [ ]

Which number has more Tens [ ] or [ ]

Which number has more Units [ ] or [ ]

Which number is *bigger* [ ] or [ ]

27

588 600

Which number has more Hundreds [ ] or [ ]

Which number has more Tens [ ] or [ ]

Which number has more Units [ ] or [ ]

Which number is *bigger* [ ] or [ ]

28

4010   4101

Which number has more Thousands ☐ or ☐

Which number has more Hundreds ☐ or ☐

Which number has more Tens ☐ or ☐

Which number has more Units ☐ or ☐

Which number is *bigger* ☐ or ☐

29

6719   7001

Which number has more Thousands ☐ or ☐

Which number has more Hundreds ☐ or ☐

Which number has more Tens ☐ or ☐

Which number has more Units ☐ or ☐

Which number is *bigger* ☐ or ☐

30

3459   1877

Which number has more Thousands ☐ or ☐

Which number has more Hundreds ☐ or ☐

Which number has more Tens ☐ or ☐

Which number has more Units ☐ or ☐

Which number is *bigger* ☐ or ☐

31

2345   3245

Which number has more Thousands   ☐   or   ☐

Which number has more Hundreds   ☐   or   ☐

Which number has more Tens   ☐   or   ☐

Which number has more Units   ☐   or   ☐

Which number is *bigger*   ☐   or   ☐

32

5792   5972

Which number has more Thousands   ☐   or   ☐

Which number has more Hundreds   ☐   or   ☐

Which number has more Tens   ☐   or   ☐

Which number has more Units   ☐   or   ☐

Which number is *bigger*   ☐   or   ☐

33

6357   6537

Which number has more Thousands   ☐   or   ☐

Which number has more Hundreds   ☐   or   ☐

Which number has more Tens   ☐   or   ☐

Which number has more Units   ☐   or   ☐

Which number is *bigger*   ☐   or   ☐

Decoding Exercises

34

Write in Expanded Form

Th H T U
7   2 5 6

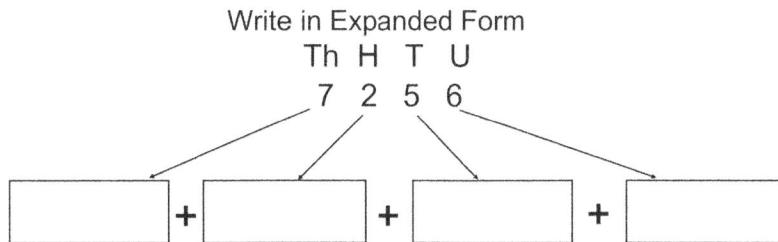

35

Write in Expanded Form

Th H T U
4   6 8 2

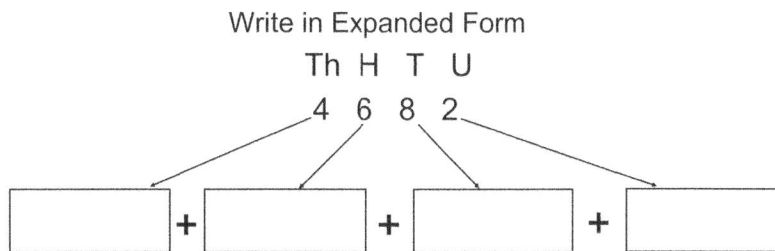

36

Write in Expanded Form

Th H T U
8   0 3 7

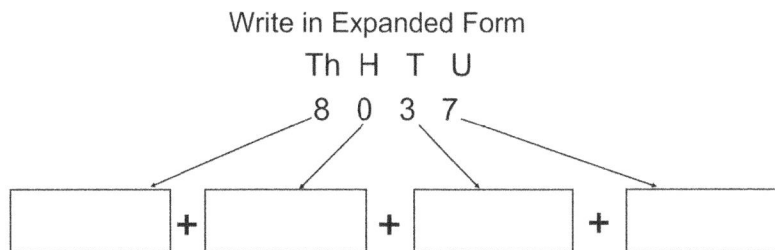

37	Write the Place Value of **5** in each of the numbers below

3 **5**82	3 82**5**	8 3**5**2	**5** 382

38

EXAMPLE

a) 4 103 — Increase by three hundred → | 4 4 0 3 |

b) 2 318 — Increase by four Tens → | |

c) 3 456 — Increase by five thousand → | |

d) 9 283 — Increase by six ones → | |

EXAMPLE

e) 2 715 — Exchange the **U** and **T** → | 2 7 5 1 |

f) 4 062 — Exchange the **Th** and **H** → | |

g) 4 136 — Increase by 5 T / Decrease by 2 H → | |

h) 7 654 — Increase by 2 H / Decrease by 2 Th → | |

i) 5 860 — Exchange the **U** and **T** → | |

j) 3 402 — Exchange the **Th** and **H** → | |

k) 6 361 — Increase by 5 T / Decrease by 2 H → | |

l) 7 128 — Decrease by 2 H / Increase by 2 Th → | |

Decoding Exercises

39

EXAMPLE

Write in Expanded Form

Th H T U
7   3 9 2

| 7 000 | + | 300 | + | 90 | + | 2 |

40

Write in Expanded Form

Th H   T   U
5   6   7   8

☐ + ☐ + ☐ + ☐

41

Write in Expanded Form

Th H   T   U
8   4   1   6

☐ + ☐ + ☐ + ☐

42

Write in Expanded Form

Th H   T   U
4   2   5   3

☐ + ☐ + ☐ + ☐

Decoding Exercises

Study the following *exchanges* carefully

EXAMPLE

Exchange
Tens and **U**nits

	Th	H	T	U
1st number	5	7	**1**	**2**
2nd number	5	7	**2**	**1**

exchange

Now fill in the empty boxes:

The 2nd number

increased ☑   decreased ☐

by

9

Th	H	T	U
			☑

Decoding Exercises

Study the following *exchanges* carefully

43   *Exchange*
Tens and Units

Th	H	**T**	**U**
1st number	3	4	**1**	**7**

exchange

| *2nd number* | 3 | 4 | **7** | **1** |

44   *Exchange*
Hudreds & Tens

Th	**H**	**T**	U
1st number	5	**7**	**1**	2

exchange

| *2nd number* | 5 | **1** | **7** | 2 |

45   *Exchange*
Thousands & Hundreds

Th	**H**	T	U
1st number	**5**	**7**	1	2

exchange

| *2nd number* | **7** | **5** | 7 | 2 |

▼

Now fill in the empty boxes:

The 2nd number

increased   decreased

☐   ☐

by

☐

Th   H   T   U
◻   ◻   ◻   ◻

▼

Now fill in the empty boxes:

The 2nd number

increased   decreased

☐   ☐

by

☐

Th   H   T   U
◻   ◻   ◻   ◻

▼

Now fill in the empty boxes:

The 2nd number

increased   decreased

☐   ☐

by

☐

Th   H   T   U
◻   ◻   ◻   ◻

46

	Th	H	T	U
1st number	4	0	7	1
2nd number	4	0	1	7

Now fill in the empty boxes:

The 2nd number

increased　　　decreased

□　　　　　□

by

□

Th	H	T	U

47

	Th	H	T	U
1st number	3	2	6	4
2nd number	3	6	2	4

Now fill in the empty boxes:

The 2nd number

increased　　　decreased

□　　　　　□

by

□

Th	H	T	U

48

	Th	H	T	U
1st number	2	9	9	8
2nd number	9	2	9	8

Now fill in the empty boxes:

The 2nd number

increased　　　decreased

□　　　　　□

by

□

Th	H	T	U

49

	Th	H	T	U
1st number	7	4	3	6
2nd number	7	4	6	3

Now fill in the empty boxes:

The 2nd number

increased　　　decreased

□　　　　　□

by

□

Th	H	T	U

50

	Th	H	T	U
1st number	5	6	9	2
2nd number	5	9	6	2

Now fill in the empty boxes:

The 2nd number

increased　　　decreased

□　　　　　□

by

□

Th	H	T	U

51

	Th	H	T	U
1st number	8	1	7	2
2nd number	1	8	7	2

Now fill in the empty boxes:

The 2nd number

increased　　　decreased

□　　　　　□

by

□

Th	H	T	U

Made in the USA
Las Vegas, NV
13 July 2024